William Boscawen

The Progress of Satire

An Essay with Notes Containing Remarks on The Pursuit of Literature.

Second Edition

William Boscawen

The Progress of Satire
An Essay with Notes Containing Remarks on The Pursuit of Literature. Second Edition

ISBN/EAN: 9783337106911

Printed in Europe, USA, Canada, Australia, Japan

Cover: Foto ©Thomas Meinert / pixelio.de

More available books at **www.hansebooks.com**

'THE

PROGRESS OF SATIRE:

AN

ESSAY IN VERSE.

WITH NOTES,

CONTAINING

REMARKS ON " THE PURSUITS OF LITERATURE."

SECOND EDITION,
WITH CONSIDERABLE ADDITIONS.

———— non fi quid turbida Roma
Elevet, accedas; examenque improbum in iftâ
Caftiges trutinâ.

What, if an addle-headed Public praife
The proud conceited Pedant's rumbling lays,
Shall we not weigh his infolent pretence
In jufter fcales,—the fcales of Truth and Senfe?

LONDON:

PRINTED FOR J. BELL, NO. 148, OXFORD-STREET.

MDCCXCVIII.

PREFACE.

THE approbation with which the following Essay has been received by * many of the best judges, and, indeed, by the public in general, has induced me to revise it with care, and endeavour, by confiderable additions and improvements, to render it more worthy of their notice. I am, however, fenfible it can claim but little

* Among thefe I could mention two, at leaft, of the four gentlemen in whofe fuppofed approbation my adverfary triumphs. But I fcorn to quote the private converfations of any man in favour of my work. It is equally unfair and mean in an anonymous writer; fince the public at large have no means of knowing whether he fpeaks truth, or not. Let that public decide (and they will decide juftly in the end), whether the *little Satirift's* Poem (as he calls it) or this Effay is written with moft candour, tafte, or even poetical fpirit.

merit

merit, except in the intention; which is, not to retaliate any perfonal infult myfelf or friends may have fuftained, but to fhew to the public, and particularly to men of literature, how unbecoming it is in itfelf, and how prejudicial to the interefts of learning, to encourage anonymous Satires; the authors of which, being fecure from all effectual refponfibility, attack indifcriminately the moft refpectable characters, and laugh at every appeal to the laws of candour and good-nature.

The reader of this who may have perufed the Letter prefixed to the later editions of the *Purfuits of Literature*, will probably be of opinion that the Author's defence (if it can be deemed one) againft the charge of perfonal malignity is chiefly directed to the objections urged againft him in this work. He difdains, indeed, to name any of his adverfaries, or to reply in detail to any one of their accufations. This is convenient: this is worthy of the GREAT AUTHOR; who, like the *Great Nation*, may condefcend to *do* an injury, but fhould never condefcend to repair, or even fairly to defend it.

But

But let him, if he dares, come to the point. Let him, inſtead of ſheltering himſelf under general expreſſions, juſtify the *inſtances* of miſconduct brought forward in this publication. If he declines to do this, may not the contempt with which he affects to treat his adverſaries (adding inſult to injury) be retorted by an indignant public on himſelf?

Adverting, however, in the mean time to the leading topics of this notable defence, let us conſider whether the principles laid down by him are not often unjuſt, and whether they are, at all events, applicable to thoſe inſtances of the writer's miſconduct which have been repeatedly produced.

" Playfulneſs and humour," he complains, " have received other appellations;" viz. (I preſume, for his *delicacy* does not permit him to name them,) ill-nature and inſolence. A few queſtions will enable the public to decide on this point.

1. Is it playfulneſs and humour (or does it deſerve thoſe *other* appellations) to blend with

A 3   the

the opinion of an Author's work a reprefenta-
tion, or rather mifreprefentation, of his private
concerns, for the purpofe of rendering his character ridiculous*? In other words, Does every
man who publifhes a book expofe *thereby* all
his private life to farcaftic obfervation and
obloquy?

2. Is it " playfulnefs and humour" to mif-
reprefent the origin and object of a charitable
inftitution, for the purpofe of ridiculing that inftitution, or fome perfon who endeavours to
promote it†?

3. Is it *mere* playfulnefs and humour (without the leaft mixture of ill-will or envy) farcaf-

* This he has done in fome inftances; and in one, perhaps,
a much heavier charge might be juftly brought againft him.
But it is referved till he fhall be *compleatly* drawn forth from
his lurking-place. He is, indeed, fufficiently known already
to all who duly confider the circumftances that have happened fince the firft publication of his work.

† See Part IV. page 13, of the early editions. It is true
this fhameful paffage is now omitted, but it ftood in two or
three editions; and the author has therefore no right to ex-
pect it fhould be forgotten.

tically

tically to depreciate the talents of a gentleman, even at the expence of truth, becaufe he has, early in life, obtained a refpectable and confidential fituation under the government of the country * ?

4. Is it *mere* playfulnefs and humour to dwell at length, farcaftically, as well as ludicroufly, on the propenfity of a man of learning (no Author by the way) to collect curious editions of books, and his attending at fales for that purpofe † ?

---

* He reprefents the *Microcofm,* to which Mr. Canning, whilft a boy at Eton, contributed, as the work of his riper years, for the purpofe of depreciating his abilities. Some circumftance, however, has alarmed or fhamed the little man, for he has fuddenly changed his fatirical note into a panegyric, and thinks the former is forgot:—

" Infolent thought ! and like a fecond blow."

† I think no candid man can doubt that his note on Dr. Goffet, (Part IV. page 13.) as it ftood at firft, was meant ill-naturedly to depreciate and ridicule him, however powerlefs in it's effect. If, as he intimates, Dr. G. laughs at the note himfelf, it is at the folly and abfurdity, not at any wit or humour, contained in it.

5. Is

5. Is it playfulnefs or humour to reprefent
the diligence of a refpectable Member of Parliament, in effecting thofe improvements in the
promulgation of Statutes, and that attention to
the revival of them the want of which has been
juftly complained of, as originating in the mere
defire of felf-importance *?

6. Is it playfulnefs and humour to endeavour
to vilify one of the brighteft ornaments of our
church, by reprefenting him as proud and mean,
on an idle tale, unfupported by evidence, and
contrary to the known liberality of his character +?

7. Is it playfulnefs and humour to pronounce
the mind of a man to be crafty, merely from the

* See Part IV. page 29, (note i.)   This wretched attempt
at ill-natured farcafm is now indeed omitted ; but I faw it in
the third edition of that Dialogue, and believe it continued
to the fifth : fo that his malice circulated throughout the
kingdom.   Nor does he now make the leaft apology.

+ The ftory arifes, I am well informed, from a circumftance that happened when the Prelate alluded to was Bifhop
of Salifbury, but without his fault.   Let the little man, if he
dares, produce his authority for the affertion he has hazarded.

appearance

appearance of his countenance in a print? and this too of a venerable exile; whofe rank, chara&ter, and misfortunes have a peculiar claim to the prote&tion of this country *?

Laftly; Is it mere playfulnefs and humour to allude, ·in farcaftic and contemptuous terms, to the circumftance of a diftinguifhed Barrifter being obliged, by the inceffant exertions of his mind and fatigues of his profeffion, to take opium occafionally for his relief +?

More inftances might be produced; but thefe may, for the prefent, be fufficient to exercife all the Author's ingenuity in defence. But I afk his pardon—this he difdains—his " ‡ *countenance*

---

* See Part IV. page 26, (note e.) A remark as ungenerous as ever difgraced the page of a libeller.

+ The whole note on Mr. Erfkine is, indeed, unworthy of any gentleman or fcholar.

‡ κυνος ομματ' εχων.—But when, foon afterwards, he declares his refolution to remain concealed, what reader does not anticipate the conclufion— κραδιην δ' ελαφοιο ?—and may we not juftly exclaim (in the ftrong language of Pope's tranflation),

Oh monfter, mix'd of infolence and fear!
Thou dog in forehead, but in heart a deer!

" *is*

" *is unaltered,*" &c. Bravo! There is nothing like facing it out: there is nothing so convenient as to avoid all discussions of a conduct which candour and justice would condemn, to ridicule the complaints of the injured, to despise the censures of the candid, and to trample on public opinion in the solemn confidence of assumed dignity.

Yet, after all, though *we* are too great to answer distinctly to any one charge, we do not find it quite safe to rest our justification on the work itself. No: the GREAT AUTHOR must descend a little from his dignity: he must throw out a few general topicks, by which the inattentive, the indolent, or the partial reader may, if possible, be misled. The quotation, for instance, of a passage from Horace, designed by it's Author to justify a single line, (which laughed at two contemptible individuals,) is applied to the justification of all ridicule, whatever it's kind or degree. But if the opinion of any satirist in his own defence can be produced as an argument, let us hear the same Poet on the subject of unwarranted and unfeeling ridicule:

—— Solutos

———— Solutos

Qui captat rifus hominum, famamque dicacis ;

Fingere qui non vifa poteſt, *commiſſa tacere*

Qui nequit, hic * *niger* eſt.

Is this, (I will aſk any candid man,) or the paſſage he has himſelf cited, moſt applicable to the Author of *The Purſuits of Literature?*

" Cenſure," he complains, " is reprefented as " malignity, and reprehenfion as abufe." Now if his cenfures appear, from the manner or degree, to arife from malignity; if his reprehenfion degenerate into abufe, who is to blame? the perfon who gives occafion for fuch charges, or he by whom they are brought? I might felect, as an inftance, his furious attack on Dr. Warton.

* I have heard the tranflation of this paffage by Francis ridiculed, as a ftrange and ludicrous departure from the original. But it now appears to have been written with a *prophetic* fpirit:

This man is vile : here, Roman, fix your mark !

His foul is black, as *his complexion's dark.*

Vol. iii. p. 61.

The whole paffage is, indeed, (in the tranflation,) not only defcriptive of the little Satirift, but very much in the general ftyle of his poetry.

I main-

" *is unaltered,*" &c. Bravo! There is nothing
like facing it out: there is nothing fo convenient
as to avoid all difcuffions of a conduct which
candour and juftice would condemn, to ridicule
the complaints of the injured, to defpife the cenfures of the candid, and to trample on public
opinion in the folemn confidence of affumed
dignity.

Yet, after all, though *we* are too great to
anfwer diftinctly to any one charge, we do not
find it quite fafe to reft our juftification on the
work itfelf. No: the GREAT AUTHOR muft
defcend a little from his dignity: he muft throw
out a few general topicks, by which the inattentive, the indolent, or the partial reader may, if
poffible, be mifled. The quotation, for inftance,
of a paffage from Horace, defigned by it's Author to juftify a fingle line, (which laughed at
two contemptible individuals,) is applied to the
juftification of all ridicule, whatever it's kind or
degree. But if the opinion of any fatirift in his
own defence can be produced as an argument,
let us hear the fame Poet on the fubject of unwarranted and unfeeling ridicule:

——— Solūtos
Qui captat rifus hominum, famamque dicacis ;
Fingere qui non vifa poteft, *commiſſa tacere*
Qui nequit, hic * *niger* eft.

Is this, (I will afk any candid man,) or the
paffage he has himfelf cited, moſt applicable to
the Author of *The Purſuits of Literature?*

" Cenfure," he complains, " is reprefented as
" malignity, and reprehenfion as abufe." Now
if his cenfures appear, from the manner or degree, to arife from malignity; if his reprehenfion
degenerate into abufe, who is to blame? the
perfon who gives occafion for fuch charges, or
he by whom they are brought? I might felect,
as an inftance, his furious attack on Dr. Warton.

* I have heard the tranflation of this paffage by Francis
ridiculed, as a ſtrange and ludicrous departure from the
original. But it now appears to have been written with a
prophetic fpirit:

This man is vile : here, Roman, fix your mark!
His foul is black, as *his complexion's dark.*

Vol. iii. p. 61.

The whole paffage is, indeed, (in the tranflation,) not only
defcriptive of the little Satiriſt, but very much in the general
ſtyle of his poetry.

I main-

I maintain that in ＊ two points his cenfure is without juſt foundation ; but, if they admit of a doubt, he ſhould have refrained from unqualified and vehement reprehenſion. In the other point, if we grant that Dr. W. miſtook his duty as Editor, is that a juſtification of infolent and brutal invective †?

A more important objection (as he admits it to be) has been brought againſt his work, as in-conſiſtent with that religion which he affects ſo much to revere. But how does our Satiriſt ſtate the objection ? Is it (as he reprefents) an ob-jection to fatire in general ? or to paltry, info-lent, uncandid, and (too often) malicious fatire? Whether *The Purſuits of Literature* deferve that character, or not, is the only point to be fettled between us. Should it be found to merit all or any of thefe appellations, I ſhould like (for once)

* See the Poſtſcript to this work.

† And this from the fame writer who, in another part of his work, ridicules Sir James Burges for not having made his Poem lafcivious and indecent ! This from the fame man who publiſhed the grofsly indecent paſſage about Acis and Galatea, and the more infamous alluſions refpecting Mr. Steevens, &c. &c. ! ! !—Oh ſhame, where is thy bluſh ?

to

to fee him lay his hand on his heart and anfwer this queftion: Have you, the pretended
champion of Chriftianity, acted on the divine
principle of " loving your neighbour as your-
" felf?" Have you (I will ftake the whole
caufe upon this iffue) invariably " *done unto*
" *others as you would that others fhould do unto*
" *you ?*"

I now proceed to the ftrong hold, the tower
of his defence. We, who condemn his work,
as (in many parts) little better than a libel, are,
it feems, deftitute, not only of common fenfe,
but (*rifum teneatis!*) of *common law :* for, behold,
the GREAT AUTHOR, he who holds Barrifters
in fuch fupreme contempt, has gone fo far in his
legal lucubrations as to confult an elementary
book: (*Calvum et doctus cantare Catullum*) protected *, as he thinks, by the authority of one
legal *dictum*, he laughs at all appeals to candour,
or to feeling, and defies the facred tribunal of

* Even this might be fairly queftioned; for that fpecies of
chaftifement which (it is admitted on all hands) the little
Satirift has fo often provoked, would certainly be a breach of
the peace, however merited. He feems alfo compleatly ignorant that the principle quoted applies only to an indict-
ment for a mifdemeanor, not an action for damages.

honour.

honour. But here my *learned friend* muft ex-
cufe me if, inftead of accepting the iffue tender-
ed, I *demur* to his plea. Can no writing, then,
be deemed, in common *parlance*, libellous, unlefs
it be indictable at law? Can no character be
depreciated, no honourable feeling wounded, no
literary injuftice effected, without the means of
legal redrefs? What other defence have the
moft malignant fcribblers, than that they juft
contrive to keep out of the pale of the law?
Let me, however, advife him, now he has feized
on this vantage ground, to reft on it, as the
moft fecure. Let him not talk of his " cha-
" racter and reputation with his country," fince
he muft be confcious how wantonly he has
fported with the characters of others: let him
not appeal to Chriftianity, as the teft of his conduct, while he muft feel that he has violated the
moft extenfive principle of Chriftian morality.

Having, in the notes to this edition, remarked
on moft of the other topics of the little Gentleman's defence, I will now only notice the convenient principle under which he would fhelter
all his illiberal attacks on individuals, all his un-
manly and unfeeling ridicule. " *When the un-*
" *derftanding*"

" *derſtanding*" (ſays he, with a Greek quotation *more ſuo*) " *is enervated, &c. it is open to all* " *manner of deception, and to all the impreſſions of* " *ſophiſtry.*" Were we to admit the truth of this principle *, in one ſenſe and in ſome degree, it would be impoſſible for the Author to prove it's. application to one half of the perſons and works which he has thought proper to ſtigmatize, or oppoſe it to the inſtances of miſconduct which have been repeatedly produced.

This, however, and all ſimilar pretences, he *knows* to be vain. Scarcely a paſſage in which he has endeavoured to teaſe and vex, or to depreciate and injure, reſpectable perſons could have been written with the view of correcting their ſuppoſed errors, or producing any real good to ſociety. No: the manifeſt object was to exhibit the pleaſantry and humour of which he believes himſelf to be poſſeſſed, and to amuſe himſelf with his vaunted power of inflicting

---

* Perhaps we might deny the principle itſelf; at leaſt in any ſenſe applicable to the point in queſtion. For it by no means follows, that, becauſe a man thinks or acts abſurdly in a particular inſtance, (and who is there free from ſuch a foible?) his whole mind and conduct in life are thereby corrupted and miſled.

pain.

pain. The political incendiaries and jacobins
are, indeed, juſtly reprobated. But this (thank
Heaven!) was requiſite, to give popularity, or
even plauſibility, to his ſatire. After all, *" he*
" may ſometimes have made his ſatire felt; but let
" not injudicious admiration miſtake the venom of
" the ſhaft for the vigour of the bow. He has ſome-
" times ſported with lucky malice; but to him
" that knows his company it is not hard to be ſar-
" caſtic in a maſk. While he walks, like JACK THE
" GIANT-KILLER, *in a coat of darkneſs, he may do*
" much miſchief with little ſtrength. Let us abſtract
" from his wit the vivacity of inſolence, and with-
" draw from his efficacy the ſympathetic favour
" of malignity; I do not ſay that we ſhall leave
" him nothing; but if we leave him only his
" merit, what will be his praiſe?"—This was
ſaid by the great Samuel Johnſon; and it was
ſaid of a writer, " the latchet of whoſe ſhoes"
the little Satiriſt " is not worthy to unlooſe *."

* The juſteſt character of the Author of the Purſuits of
Literature was written above a hundred years ago: *Homo,*
ut notiſſimum eſt, ingenii maligni et oris maledicentiſſimi, qui,
propter præſtantiſſimorum et de re literariâ optimè meritorum
virorum invidas ac injurioſas calumniationes, merito CANIS
GRAMMATICUS *appellatur.*

ADVER-

PROGRESS OF SATIRE.

" BOLD was the man" (*a*) (as ancient Poets fay)
" Whofe feeble bark firft plough'd the wat'ry way."
As bold the Bard, who, panting for renown,
Dares launch *his* veffel on that fea—the Town ;
Nor dreads a faction's rage, a rival's fpite,
Or Satire's wanton malice (*b*) veil'd in night.

Yet

(*a*) Hor. Ode iii. Lib. I.

(*b*) The practice of ridiculing individuals by *name* in a fatirical poem, and concealing that of the author who attacks them, is equally unworthy of a fcholar and a gentleman. The writer who affails another in his perfonal, or even literary, character, fhould (if he pretends to candour) make himfelf refponfible for the juftice of his accufation.—" No :" (fays the little anonymous Satirift) " Satire never has *its full force* if the author of it is known ; for the " unworthinefs of any man leffens the ftrength of his objections.

B

" This,"

Yet bolder he who, scorning fashion's power,

Ne'er chas'd the gaudy meteors of an hour,

On native worth could build his honest claim,

And, self-supported, climb the steep of Fame. 10

Fir'd by such hopes immortal Milton sung:

Such genuine numbers flow'd from Thomson's tongue,

When, at his call, in fancy's brightest hue,

All nature rose majestick to his view.

Thus, Shakspear, master of the human heart!

Thy generous soul disdain'd each groveling art,

With fleeting shadows ne'er debas'd the stage,

But bade thy pictures live through every age.

" This," he adds, " is a full answer to all who require the name of
" a satirical Poet."——A notable answer indeed!—Not to inquire,
as I might justly do, whether the fact itself be not very question-
able; (for the candid part of mankind will surely give more credit
to accusations from a known good man than from one who *may be*
of an opposite character) what is this but to justify every species of
concealment and circumvention; which are, in many cases, more
effectual than open attacks? Would not such a doctrine protect from
censure the dark assassin and the midnight murderer? the stiletto of
the Italian, and the poisoned dart of the Indian? We now begin
to understand the *profound,* but seemingly harmless, remark, that "*the*
" *authorized*" (i. e. lawful) " *instruments of lawful war are lawful.*"
Pulchrè! benè! rectè!—The end, it seems, justifies the means!
Evil may be done that good (and a very doubtful good) may en-
sue!—Truly the little gentleman (I beg pardon, the little *man*, and
that too is scarcely a proper term,) has been well denominated *a
Jesuit.*

Yet Bards, though lefs fublime, have learn'd to pleafe
By fprightly fancy, or by graceful eafe,   20
On tafte, on feeling, true delight imprefs'd,
Nor wak'd one ranc'rous paffion in the breaft.
Thus later ages have confpir'd to praife
The courtly Waller's fmooth and gentle lays:
Thus Prior's ftrains could every grace admit:
His fertile genius, and his varied wit,
Now with love's thrilling notes the heart affail,
Now charm the fancy by fome fportive tale.
Let the true Bard, when genuine ardours rife,
Beam on his foul, and fparkle in his eyes,   30
Each fenfe, each feeling, waken'd to delight,
O'er wide creation throw his piercing fight,
View Nature's form fublime, her beauteous face,
That awes by dignity, or charms by grace,
Or trace, through each condition of mankind,
The ftrong, but varying features of the mind.
Each fcene, where'er enraptur'd Fancy ftrays,
Deck'd by her charms, infpires the Poet's lays.

Whence then does Genius, fkill'd alone to gain
The choiceft bleffings of th'Aonian train,   40

          Each

Each nobler fong, each gentler lay, decline,
Lur'd by the leaft attractive of the Nine?
In petty wars his fpendid powers difplay,
And dwell on themes that fcarce outlive the day?
Alas! 'tis envy prompts, or anger fways
Our hearts, more prone to cenfure than to praife.
Though oft th' unblufhing vices of her age
Have juftly wak'd indignant Satire's rage,
How oft does wanton wit, or ranc'rous pride,
Flow with a noxious and polluted tide,   50
Where malice tinges her envenom'd dart,
That fixes deep, and rankles in the heart!

  Arife! thy violated rights defend,
Propitious Candour, merit's conftant friend!
Averfe to mark, reluctant to accufe,
The venial faults and frailties of the Mufe,
Yet prompt to crufh each infolent pretence
By manly reafon and refiftlefs fenfe,
With generous zeal the fophift's art expofe,
And wake th' indignant ftrain 'gainft virtue's foes, 60
But, when true genius lights its heaven-born flame,
Fan the bright fparks, and point the way to fame.

                       Say,

Say, (c) fhall I paint, in fierce difdainful rhyme,

The weak, but harmlefs Poet's *deadly crime*,

And lafh the culprit, whofe afpiring lays

Strive for the nobleft meed, ingenuous praife?

Or, in conceit and pedantry's fond dream,

Make the (d) *Purfuits of Lit'rature* my theme,

Alarm the church and ftate in ftyle myfterious,

(" *Seeming humility and tone imperious*,")   70

Talk (e) "'*bout*" French priefts and Winchefter great
          houfe,

Labour like mountains, then bring forth a moufe,

Difdain

(c) This vehemence againft fome writers who were fair, though
perhaps not very fuccefsful, candidates for fame, is, in my opinion,
the fault of the Baviad. It is a departure from the Author's plan ;
which was to ridicule the arrogance and falfe tafte of a particular fet
of coxcombs. Mr. G.'s imitator, the *Purfuer of Literature*, (as
he has been juftly called) can copy only his fault, with fcarcely a
fpark of his merit.

(d) I fhould here apologize for fome clumfy abbreviations, but
that they are fanctioned by my *great* original (*errare cum Platone*,
&c.). The reader will obferve I have borrowed fome expreffions
and one entire line from him, deeming them peculiarly *happy* in
themfelves, as well as applicable to the fubject.—It is not, perhaps,
eafy to fay how *feeming humility* and *tone imperious* can exift together. But if it be meant that the general tone is imperious, with
fome occafional pretences to humility, nothing can more exactly
defcribe the Purfuits of Literature.

(e) " Of Lorkin's diligence '*bout* Lord's arrears." See P. of L.
Part Iſt, page 23, of the early editions.—The little man has in

this

. Difdain all order, and reject all plan,

Affect the fcholar, but " *forget the man*,"

(*f*) And, while détraction's dæmons " *round me roll*,"

" Stamp on th' infernal page the malice of my foul."

No : be it mine to ftem vain fafhion's tide,

That buoys the faucy fat'rift's fenfelefs pride,

And bid him, ere this angry ftrain we hear,

To his own faults be juft, if not fevere. 80

Since then, ingenuous Mufe, thy tuneful choir

For harfher founds rejects the gentle lyre,

Say, from what fource, in what far diftant age,

Fierce Satire rofe, and taught thy verfe to rage ;

Trace the ftrong current of her claffic ftrains

From ancient Rome to Britain's favour'd plains;

this, as in many other inftances, profited by my admonition, and it
now ftands—" *for* Lord's arrears !"—But perhaps the line has loft
as much in one way, by the change, as it has gained in the other.

(*f*) " And, while the fwelling numbers round him roll,
  " Stamps on th' immortal page the vifions of his foul."
                                        P. of Lit. Part IV.
The Alexandrine line, though in fome meafure copied from Dryden,
is certainly a fine one, but dearly purchafed by the admiffion of it's
bombaft affociate.—I have no ambition to become perfonally ac-
quainted with the little gentleman, but fhould like, for once, to
fee him with his pen in his hand and " the fwelling *numbers rolling*
" *round him.*"

                                        Mark

Mark where fhe breaks or truth's or candour's laws,
And wake her flumb'ring zeal in virtue's caufe.

Though far from Helicon's more tranquil fhade,
(g) Greece early nurtur'd this ungentle maid,　　90
When, fired by wrath, in keen Iambick fongs,
The bold Archilochus avenged his wrongs,
And Comick bards, with malice unconfin'd,
Affail'd the beft and wifeft of mankind;
Till juftice, waked at length, with wholefome pains
Check'd the wild licence of their favage ftrains,
Bade harfh unfeeling ribaldry to ceafe,
Nor wanton infults wound domeftick peace.
Thence taught, (h) Aurunca's Bard expos'd to view
Thofe forms his rough but vigorous pencil drew,　100

(g) Both Horace and Quintilian afcribe the origin of Satire to
the Romans: and this is true in the fenfe in which they ufed the
term; viz. to defcribe certain poems, of a mifcellaneous kind, on
the manners or morals of the times. But in modern language all
lampoons, or fevere writings, are called Satires; and the origin of
thefe may be traced to the Iambicks of Archilochus, and the old
Greek Comedy; from which laft, Horace himfelf admits, the Satires
of Lucilius were derived, with no other change than that of the
metre.

(h) Lucilius was born at Aurunca, a town of Etruria, and is
therefore called by Juvenal *Auruncæ alumnus.*

B 4　　　　　　In

In fmoother numbers and a ftyle lefs rude,
Though carelefs ftill, old Ennius' fteps purfued.
Oft as with ardent zeal he wak'd the lay,
Vice fhrunk abafh'd, and own'd the Mufe's fway;
Pale, as when Jove's avenging thunders roll,
Guilt heard, and trembled to her inmoft foul.
Yet, fam'd Lucilius, (*i*) faction's bitter rage
Could warp from candour thy diftinguifh'd page,
And zeal or intereft urg'd thee to oppofe
With angry taunts thy patron's nobleft foes.   110
But when were party's furious zealots known
To cherifh (*k*) " virtue and her friends alone ?"
Yet who the grateful tribute can refufe
To him whofe worth infpired the fweeteft Mufe ?

(*i*) Metellus is faid to have been fatirized by Lucilius; and, though
it is not clear which of the Metelli is meant, yet as the Chiefs of
that family were on bad terms with Scipio, the patron of that
Poet, there is too much reafon to think he was influenced by party
motives.

(*k*) " *Uni æquus virtuti atque ejus amicis.*" Hor.—But of what
Satirift can this be truly faid ? Certainly not of Pope, who applies the line to himfelf: (" To virtue only and her friends a
friend.") Probably Horace and his fucceffors deferved this praife
more than any of our Englifh Satirifts, excepting Young; as not
one of the names whom they attacked has been tranfmitted to us,
through other channels, as undeferving of the ftigma affixed to
them.

Horace,

Horace, thy gay yet philofophick ftrains
Nor envy warps, nor wanton malice ftains.
In thee what different charms unite to pleafe !
The fcholar's judgment with the courtier's eafe,
With graceful raillery, with wit refined
That gently probes, yet never wounds the mind. 120
To life, to manners true, thy moral page
Difplays the genuine features of the age;
And, when fome parafite, buffoon, or knave,
Some fhamelefs prodigal, or upftart flave,
Was mark'd by ridicule, thy happy art
Seem'd not to aim, yet fix'd th' unerring dart.

But angry Satire, in fucceeding times,
Awaked to vengeance, roufed by daring crimes,
When from the (*l*) Stoic fchool grave Perfius brought
The rigid lore her ancient fages taught,   130
And ardent virtue with fublimer rage
Infpired fierce Juvenal's indignant page.
What keen reproach, (alas !) what cauftick lays
Could brand too deeply (*m*) Rome's degen'rate days,

(*l*) Perfius was educated by Cornutus the philofopher, and ad-
dreffes one of his Satires to him.

(*m*) Perfius defcribed the reign of Nero, Juvenal that of Domitian.
When

When vice, the curb of fear or fhame unknown,
Rear'd her proud creft triumphant on the throne ?

From thefe illuftrious models (*n*) Britain draws
The moral fong, and frames her Satire's laws :
But to new themes her Mufe applies the rhyme,
Free as her fons, and varying as her clime.   140
To life, to manners, now no more confined,
The general faults or follies of mankind,
For bolder flights proud Satire plumes her wings,
(*o*) The friend, or foe, of Statefmen and of Kings,
And oft, with Faction's fierce refentment warm,
Points her dread vengeance, and " directs the ftorm."

  Rough Donne, in homely ftrains, devoid of art,
Spoke the plain truths that prove an honeft heart.

  (*n*) I have not deemed it neceffary to infert any account of the
French Satirifts, fince they, as well as our own, (for the moft part,)
copied from the Romans; and this Effay profeffes only to trace the
progrefs and ftate of abufes of that fpecies of poetry, not to cha-
racterize all who excelled in it.

  (*o*) Political Satire (I mean that of which the primary object is
politics) feems to have originated in this country, and cannot, perhaps, be traced higher than Butler. I had omitted to mention his
celebrated work, on account of it's fingular nature, and it's not
being derived from the Roman Satire.

                                                                    In

In learning rich, in native humour bold,

His merry tale the laughing Butler told,   150

And mark'd fanatic pride and factious zeal

In satire faithful to his country's weal.

But Dryden's vigorous Muse, as interest sways,

Now wounds by satire, and now sooths by praise:

Now stoops to crush (*p*) an envious Poet's name,

The dull proud rival of his splendid fame,

Now (*q*) weaves the mystic fable, to expose

Dire faction's arts and brand a monarch's foes.

Oh! hadst thou scorn'd thy towering soul to bend,

Of guilt the flatterer, and of vice the friend,   160

Ill-fated Bard! how few, with generous pride,

Assail'd by want, can stem corruption's tide?

How few, when life is cruel fortune's sport,

Could shun the gay allurements of a Court?

'Tis thus the pitying Muse her wrath allays,

And half forgives the strain she dares not praise.

But who thy finish'd beauties can display,

Pope, mighty master of the moral lay?

(*p*) In his Mackflecknoe.

(*q*) It is hardly necessary to say, that his Absalom and Achito-
phel is here alluded to.

Whose

Whose manly wit and polish'd taste combine,
Point the strong sense, and tune th' harmonious line.
Soft as the strains that grac'd th' Horatian lyre, 171
Sublime as Juvenal's more vigorous fire,
Thy magic numbers with prevailing art
Steal on th' enraptured ear, and win the heart.
(r) Each form succeeding Bards for Satire choose
Springs from thy various, thy accomplish'd Muse;
Whether they claim (s) just imitation's praise,
And classick thoughts adapt to British lays,
Or, more inventive, in appropriate rhymes
(t) Display the manners, and record the times, 180
Or, mighty trifles studious to rehearse,
(u) Strut on the stilts of mock-heroic verse,

(r) It is not meant that we had no examples of these different species of Satire prior to the writings of Pope, but that most of our subsequent Satirists, in these different branches, have taken him for their model.

(s) His Imitations of Horace have served as a model for all subsequent imitators.

(t) His Ethic Epistles afford the favourite example of that kind of Satire.

(u) The Rape of the Lock is here alluded to.

Or

Or (*v*) dafh proud dulnefs from Parnaffus' height,
And with the Mufe's arms affert the Mufe's right.

Alas'! could wit, could genius bright as thine
E'er give to fpleen one harfh ungenerous line;
Or bid with bitter eloquence to flow
That verfe (*x*) " which made an Addifon thy foe ?"

With wit that elfe had claim'd an equal prize,
But tafte lefs juft, fee (*y*) virtuous Young arife !   190
His keen remark, well-temper'd, though fevere,
His lively fentence, and his pointed fneer,

(*v*) The Dunciad belongs both to the third fpecies of Satire here
mentioned, and alfo to the fourth, viz. Satirical Criticifm.

(*x*) ".Curft be that verfe, how fmooth foe'er it flow,
" That tends to make one honeft man my foe!"
was the juft imprecation of Pope on malevolent Satire.   Yet too
many inftances of fpleen and ill-humour (not to fay ill-nature)
might be given from his works.   I have chofen his attack on Addifon, becaufe it originated in flight and probably ill-founded fuf-
picions, and becaufe the character of Addifon, and the important
fervice he had rendered to the morals (as well as manners) of his
country, fhould have protected him againft a treatment fo fevere.

(*y*) Scarcely any Englifh Poet is fo invariably zealous in the
caufe of virtue as Dr. Young.

At

At general vice, or flagrant follies, aim
Their nobler fting, nor wound one honour'd name.

But foon 'twas thine to mark, indignant Mufe,
Degen'rate Satire warp'd by party views.
See, her bold front Malignity difplay,
And Faction triumph (z) in fierce Churchill's lay !
Nor Candour's voice, nor fenfe of right and wrong,
Checks in it's courfe his dire vindictive fong.   200
He deals on every fide the fatal blow,
Nor owns fenfe, wit or virtue in a foe.
And yet infulted Candour muft admire,
Diftinguifh'd Bard, thy Mufe's ftrength and fire,
Muft own, if party-zeal had ne'er confined
To tranfient themes thy bold and fervid mind,
Britain had dwelt with rapture on thy page,
Preferv'd by genuine worth from age to age.

(z) Churchill feems to have been, in the ftricteft fenfe, a party
Poet, perhaps the leaft amiable votary of the Mufes. The afperity
of his Satire (often arifing from party prejudice) muft be difgufting
to every impartial reader.—Yet his poetry, though occafionally
negligent, poffeffed great vigour and fpirit : and he is lefs read at
prefent, only becaufe he chofe temporary and evanefcent fubjects for
his Satire.

Still Satire feeks a tranfitory name,

Nor heeds the call of never-dying fame,　　　210

Purfues vain fhadows, and exerts her power

To catch the fleeting fafhions of an hour.

Shrouded in night, the feign'd (a) Macgregor pours

The tide of fong from wit's abundant ftores,

Skill'd to combine with humour's richeft vein

The pomp of verfe, the mock majeftic ftrain.

And thou, fweet Bard ! o'er whofe untimely urn

The Graces droop, the Mufe delights to mourn,

(b) Tickell, in vain to tafte, to genius dear,

Accept this fond, this tributary tear !　　　220

'Twas thine by playful ridicule to feize

(c) Gay Fafhion's follies, yet her vot'ries pleafe,

(a) The name affumed by the unknown author of the Epiftle to
Sir William Chambers.

(b) Richard Tickell, Efq. grandfon to Thomas Tickell the Poet,
and friend of Addifon. The " little Satirift" calls Mr. Tickell
" the happieft occafional writer of his day." This is a juft charader;
though we may fairly fufpect the writer's motive. (*Virtutem in-
columem odimus, fublatam ex oculis quærimus invidi.*)—But Mr.
Tickell might have obtained much higher praife, had he employed
his talents in works of a more permanent nature.

(c) See *The Wreath of Fafhion* ; a poem written to ridicule the
then prevailing tafte for fentimental poetry.

Stern

(*d*) Stern Party's rage by fprightly wit allay,

And cheer her gloomy fcenes by fancy's ray.

Oh ! hadft thou e'er, by true ambition fired,

To nobler themes, to lafting fame, afpired,

Each charm, each gift of the propitious Nine,

That graced th' Aufonian fays, had beam'd in thine.

Severer Satire, from a different fource,

Flow'd with rough vehemence and turbid courfe. 230

When (*e*) C—s from Fafhion's heavenly region fell,

Enraged he waked the Majefty of Hell,

And bade him, iffuing from th' infernal gloom,

Record diftinguifh'd guilt, and ftamp it's doom.

Harfh was his cenfure, not unjuft his aim ;

(*f*) While Satire echoed the loud voice of fame.

(*d*) *The Project*, a political poem, and the witty and elegant Epiftle from Mr. Fox, Partridge-fhooting, to Mr. (now Lord John) Townfhend, Cruizing, are here alluded to ; though Mr. Tickell was moft known by his celebrated pamphlet, *Anticipation.*—His leffer poems alfo have great merit, either for wit and humour, or tendernefs and elegance :

> *His faltem accumulem donis, et fungar inani*
> *Munere.*

(*e*) Author of The Diaboliad, and fome other Poems of the fame kind, the fatire of which being merely perfonal, is now almoft wholly forgotten.

(*f*) The characters expofed in The Diaboliad were, for the moft part, notorioufly profligate.

But

But lo! what tumults rife? what buftling throng
Provokes the fcornful critic's angry fong?
'Tis (*g*) Affectation's motley crew invades,
With fteps unhallow'd, the Pierian fhades :   240
They feize the facred chair, their (*h*) fhrill notes raife,
And ring th' unvarying peal of mutual praife.
Mourn, claffic Mufe! conceit pollutes thy ftrain,
Proud *Nonfenfe* triumphs in her Crufca's reign :
When fee, refentment fparkling in his eyes,
To crufh thy foes indignant (*i*) G——d rife !
Thy foes, the fluttering infects of an hour,
Fly from his rage, or bow beneath his power.
Yet why, victorious champion, why abufe
The cheap and eafy conqueft of thy Mufe?   250
Infult the fall'n, or brand fome Bards who claim
No proud diftinction in the ranks of fame?
The modeft Poet's unobtrufive lays
True candour pardons where it cannot praife.

(*g*) Della Crufca, Anna Matilda, &c. &c. &c. who furfeited us
with their bad tafte, conceit, and effrontery : although fome of them
were not wholly deftitute of genius and poetical fpirit.

(*h*) This was a favourite mode of rhythm with the Crufca
fchool.

(*i*) Author of the Baviad and Mæviad.

Conceit

Conceit once check'd, let angry warfare ceafe,
And unoffending dullnefs reft in peace.

Or feek the nobler praife of him who draws
His pen in Virtue's and Religion's caufe,
And mark, what awful fcenes, what deeds, confpire
To roufe the Patriot's zeal, the Poet's fire !   260
See the cool Sophift, with collected mind,
Spread poifon, rage, deftruction o'er mankind !
See bafe Oppreffion, uncontroll'd by fhame,
In Freedom's garb, ufurping Freedom's name !
See, Britain, thy (*k*) triumphant flag unfurl'd !
Thy fons undaunted, " 'midft a falling world !"
And oh, while yet thy generous bands maintain
True freedom's empire o'er the circling main,
Senfe, learning, genius, in thy caufe unite !
Be bold in eloquence, as firm in fight !   270
" (*l*) Senfe, genius, learning, wit, in me combine,"
A *namelefs fat'rift* cries, " all, all are mine !
" 'Tis mine, by keen unerring judgment graced,
" To reign, defpotic arbiter of tafte,

(*k*) Thefe lines were written immediately after the news of Lord Duncan's glorious victory.

(*l*) No impartial reader of *The Purfuits of Literature* will, I think, deem the following fpeech exaggerated, notwithftanding the veil of modefty occafionally affumed by the Author.

" To

" To awe by (*m*) myſtic threats the paſſive Town,

" Raiſe by a ſmile, extinguiſh by a frown,

" And brand the name of each devoted wight,

" But hide my own, (*n*) ſecured by friendly night."

Alas!

(*m*) In one of his Prefaces (viz. to Part II. edit. 1ſt.) the *little great Author* ſays, " I diſſuade every perſon from flippant and ran- " dom application of any ſuppoſed name: it is as unjuſt as it is ab- " ſurd. *Flebit, et inſignis totá cantabitur urbe,* was ſaid of old; and " I recommend to every gentleman and lady of eminent ſagacity " and curioſity, to remember that there is a darkneſs *which may be* " *felt.*" In his Preface to Part IV. he uſes expreſſions which, to all *common* apprehenſions, ſeem equivalent: viz. that " *it will be more* " *than fooliſh* to be very inquiſitive."

The audacious preſumption of the above threat could only be equalled by its egregious abſurdity. No man, I believe, read it without a mixture of indignation and contempt. But, when laſh'd, on that account, in this and ſome other publications, what does the little gentleman reply?—Truly, that no threat was intended!—It was meant only to intimate that ſuch an attempt would be fruit- leſs. Wiſely, however, he omits the firſt and ſtrongeſt of the two paſſages; a paſſage to which it is impoſſible, by any torture of ex- preſſions, to give a different meaning. The latter, indeed, is plain enough; eſpecially as he took care to print the moſt material words in *Italicks*. What are we now to think of this *high and mighty* champion of morality, religion, &c.; who (as a great writer ex- preſſes it) " meanly ſneaks out of a difficulty, into which he had " proudly ſtrutted?"

(*n*) Yet he boaſts of his courage (See the concluding Note to Part IV.), that courage which dares not look the injured in the face! He might as well pride himſelf on his character; that cha-

C 2
racter

Alas ! can pride to such importance raise

A wretched mortal, puff'd by transient praise ?   280

Thou, who (o) no faults, no weakness, canst excuse,

Hear thy own merits from th' ingenuous Muse ;

Who, proud all just distinctions to admit,

Proclaims thee half a Poet, (p) half a Wit ;

Now

racter which shuns the test of scrutiny ! But I ask his pardon :— " *The unworthiness of any man lessens the strength of his ob-*" *jections.*" This curious defence has been already exposed. But it is something to find it admitted there may be some *unworthiness* even in THE GREAT AUTHOR. I am apt, indeed, to suspect we should find him to be a poor mortal, like ourselves, liable to all our prejudices, impelled by our passions, and indulging some of the worst of them. The objection, however, to anonymous Satire on private characters (and even on literary works, unless you fairly discuss them) is, I conceive, unanswerable. Every accuser ought to be responsible, if not for the truth, at least for the fairness of his charge, and the integrity of his motives. An anonymous Satirist is " an unknown Prosecutor." He shrinks from that responsibility to which every man who attacks the character of another ought to subject his own.

(o) He dwells on the slightest faults of eminent writers with an invidious minuteness, slightly noticing their merits, or (in some cases) passing them over entirely.

(p) Although the person alluded to is, no doubt, concerned in the work, it is next to impossible the whole should have been written by one person ; not so much from a variety in the style, as from the strange and frequent inconsistencies throughout. It is scarcely ever, indeed, elegant, but sometimes it has a certain degree of poetical
spirit :

Now vig'rous, fpirited, (*q*) almoft fublime,

Now tagging (*r*) feeble words to feeble rhyme ;

Now

fpirit : at other times it is not only profaic, but vulgar ; though no
one is fo forward as the writer in cenfuring every degree of vulgarity in others. Sometimes his declamations in the Notes appear
eloquent, at others frothy and puerile : on fome occafions his far-
cafms are pointed and juft ; on others wretchedly trifling, or de-
liberately ill-natured.

(*q*) In his moft laboured effort at fublimity (Part IV. from page
15 to 22 of the firft edition,) he is in part fuccefsful ; but in fome
parts inflated and obfcure. There is alfo too much appearance of
art and labour. The writer refembles, as Johnfon (and, I think,
Longinus before him) expreffed it, " a lion kindling his rage by the
" lafh of his own tail." True fublimity is more fimple and natural.
I had remark'd that his poet, who

Hears in each blaft fome confecrated rhyme,

Trac'd by the fpirit of the troublous clime,

muft have been the noted *Della Crufca.* He has now omitted the
couplet, but without fubftituting any thing to connect that which
preceded to that which followed it ; which now appear disjointed,
and little better than nonfenfe. And we have ftill " *the fwelling*
" *numbers round him roll,*" nearly as bombaft an expreffion, I venture
to fay, as ever was hazarded in poetry.

(*r*) To cite the feeble and profaic paffages in *The Purfuits of
Literature,* would be to repeat almoft half the book. Many alfo,
which are not quite profaic, are inelegant and vulgar ; and the
purity and propriety of the Englifh language are often grofsly
violated : a fault unpardonable in one who affumes the office of a
fatirical critic and literary cenfor. Some of thefe improprieties he

C 3

has

Now arm'd, 'gainſt daring crimes, in Virtue's cauſe,
Now meanly cavilling at (*s*) petty flaws;

Now

has lately correﬅed; inﬅruﬅed (as it ſhould ſeem) by *The Progreſs
of Satire;* though he has not the gratitude to confeſs his obliga-
tion. His dogs no longer wear *blue ſandals,* nor are they " *coated
" for the public brunt."* But they are ﬅill " *black-letter'd for a
" ſpace:"* for the *joke* of printing the word in black-letter could
not be ſpared. The other improprieties remain, with many that
had not been noticed; yet this edition, he ſays, has been reviſed
with the greateſt care. Many of his vulgarities are noticed in a
very ſenſible eſſay called *Striﬅures on the Purſuits of Literature.*
Many more, and perhaps ﬅronger, inﬅances might be added.—But,
" *Le jeu ne vaut pas la chandelle."* I will, therefore, only remind
my little *friend* (againﬅ his next reviſion) of the chimney-ſweeper's
reply to Pope:—" *Mend you! It would take leſs trouble to make a
" new one."*

(*s*) What can be more paltry, than the cavils he makes at the
commentators on Shakeſpeare; than his ſarcaſms on the profeſſion
and private concerns of writers (with which neither he nor the public
has any thing to do); on Mr. Erſkine for taking opium; on Mr.
Abbot for having a ſmiling countenance, &c. &c.?—" He ﬅoops to
" ſuch trifles" (he would have us believe) " rather unwillingly."
Quite the reverſe, if the *evidentia rei* is to decide. Nothing appears
to delight him ſo much: he is never in his own element but when he
can indulge in this kind of ribaldry. But has this child of " play-
" fulneſs and humour" (as he is pleaſed to term his wanton and
unfeeling ridicule) never read the fable of the Boys and Frogs? Does
he really think it allowable to depreciate the charaﬅers and ſport with
the feelings of reſpeﬅable perſons, *merely to obtain a greater variety of
topics for his ſatire?* His defence, in effeﬅ, amounts to this, and this
alone—(See the Letter to a Friend, prefixed to The P. of L., 7th
edit.

Now candid, now by prejudice debafed,

(A (*t*) Bigot's principles, a (*u*) Pedant's tafte)   296

Prompt

edit. p. 12.)—I leave it to the judgment which every man of candour and feeling muft pronounce. With regard to the " high " crime and mifdemefnor" which fome fcholars have committed by tranflating Gray's Elegy, the little gentleman bears teftimony againft himfelf, when he afks " What intereft have mankind in a " few old Greek boys in gowns and caffocks?" Then pray, my good Sir, why all thefe remarks upon them? Why dwell on the fubject through fourteen pages of text and notes? But " the ex- " ample," it feems, " *is of the deepeft confequence.*" Indeed! Thefe Greek *boys* are then become men of fuch eminence as to poifon by this *dreadful* example the whole current of literature. How inconfiftent does a writer become when he ceafes to make truth and candour his guides!

(*t*) If his furious and inceffant declamations againft the unfortunate French Priefts, and his ridiculous fears left our charitable fupport of them fhould endanger the Eftablifhed Church, do not flamp him *a Bigot*, any argument to prove the point muft be thrown away. " All he has advifed" (he tells us) " is on the fide of cau- " tion." Be it fo. But what occafion then for mifreprefentation and invective? If this be the language of caution, what is that of perfecution? What could he have faid more, had his defign been to excite every vindictive paffion againft thefe refpectable men, who are the martyrs, not to the Roman Catholic perfuafion, but to Chriftianity itfelf?

(*u*) If pedantry be properly defined " an oftentatious difplay of " learning," no one but a pedant can deny the little Gentleman that title. I had quoted a ftrong inftance of it, his quaint and forced conceit (continued through ten pages) of comparing the Commentators on Shakefpeare to Actæon's hounds. But inftances might be produced from almoft every page. What he fays in de-

Prompt to repel Religion's barbarous foes,

Yet (*x*) crush her sons, and aggravate their woes;

And

fence of his quotations, does not apply to those instances (and they are numerous) where the quotations are needless to illustrate the subject, or where they are drawn from Authors little known and of little merit or weight. Nor does he, in general, give the substance of them in English, as he is pleased to assert.

(*x*) It is matter of great surprise to me that the candid and able writer of "*Strictures on the Pursuits of Literature*" should acquiesce in the illiberal invectives on the Emigrant Priests. He seems not to have considered against *whom* those invectives were directed, and upon what grounds. The Emigrants at large are not persecuted by the little Satirist; nor are their *political* principles adverted to. No: he affects to fear only the helpless, the respectable body of men, against whose *general* conduct in this kingdom slander itself has scarcely ventured a whisper; against whom the Author himself does not bring any specific charge. The charges that were brought by others were, I am well informed, refuted by a diligent and dispassionate inquiry.—While they were maintained at Winton, they were placed (says he) "on a hill," meaning (if he has any rational meaning) to object to their conspicuous situation, and to their being maintained in a body, instead of being dispersed in private houses; the very circumstances, I conceive, that most effectually prevented the dissemination of their religious principles. When they had been removed from that asylum, even this did not satisfy the malice of their persecutor. He discovered, it seems, that they were still allowed, though in smaller parties, to associate together. This was sufficient to excite another furious philippic. The *mode* of relief is also objected to; although it is administered under the direction of a Committee of respectable Gentlemen, and known friends to our Established Church; and the Bishop of Leon is only consulted as best knowing, the characters and pretensions of those who apply. But if there is no intention to deprive these helpless

objects

And blending love of truth and zeal for right
With bloated *(y)* arrogance, and *(z)* envious fpite.

Nor

objects of charitable fupport, why is the fum allotted to them and the Lay Emigrants (who are on this occafion joined in order to inflame the reckoning) fo frequently ftated and invidioufly dwelt upon ? He cannot be ignorant that, whatever may be the aggregate amount, the pittance to each individual is barely adequate to the fuftenance of life. But what if, in addition to this, it fhould appear *from the Records of Parliament* that the whole fum hitherto granted for the fupport of the Emigrants amounts to lefs than he has ftated as granted in the year 1796 ALONE ?—I leave every reader to draw the inference.—To fay " GOVERNMENT ought not to relieve them," is to fay they fhould not be relieved at all; the funds of private charity having been long fince exhaufted.

(y) The proofs of his arrogance (I repeat it) ftare the Reader in the face in almoft every page ; though we have here and there an hypocritical profeffion of humility. The very purpofe of his work (viz. to exalt or deprefs the fame of cotemporary writers at his will and pleafure) is the height of arrogance. It is fomething worfe, to decline contemptuoufly a difcuffion of thofe charges which are brought againft him by refpectable and injured perfons, and echoed by the almoft unanimous voice of mankind. " The *fume fuperbiam* of a Poet ought not (he tells us) to be rigidly " examined." But (befides that it appears full as often in his profe) it ought to be the pride of a *real* Poet, not of one whofe poetry (excepting a few occafional fallies) confifts chiefly of flat and profaic lines, or inelegancies and improprieties of language, or fervile, unacknowledged, and, for the moft part, clumfy, imitations of Pope.

(z) How far his attacks on meritorious writers originate in envy, is beft known to his own heart; but if moft of thofe which I have inftanced are not *fpiteful,* I know not what can be

deemed

Nor think, howe'er she boaſt her motley rhymes,

Thy (*a*) ſhapeleſs Muſe ſhall live to after-times.

No : though ſuſtain'd by mean unworthy art,

She (*b*) feed each baſer paſſion of the heart,

Indignant

deemed ſo. He bluſters, indeed, in his *Letter to a Friend*, as if he was, in every caſe, juſtifiable. But how does this boaſt accord with his frequent, though ſilent, retractions? If the paſſages in queſtion were at firſt proper, he ſhould not afterwards have omitted them in compliance with any cenſure. To give a ſtriking inſtance : The diſparaging account of Mr. Canning (manifeſtly the offſpring of envy) is now, by a magic touch of the pen, converted into praiſe, and without the leaſt apology or explanation. The candid acknowledgment of error might indeed, in ſome degree, atone for it. But this attempt to deceive our memories, this ſilent tergiverſation, is the diſgraceful ſubterfuge of meanneſs and inſolence.

. (*a*) I call his Muſe *ſhapeleſs*, becauſe *nec pes nec caput uni reddatur formæ.* Indeed the whole paſſage in Horace deſcribes a work ſimilar to *The Purſuits of Literature.* The Author ſays he could analyſe his work ; but I am convinced he dares not attempt it : for ſuch a proceſs would ſhew it in all it's native deformity. The authority of Pope's two Dialogues will not avail him. For (beſides that their merit would cover moſt defects) they are much ſhorter poems, and on a ſingle ſubject, his own writings; and they contain, in ſubſtance, merely a defence of himſelf, however occaſionally illuſtrated by general topics. But in far the greater part of Pope's ſatirical works there is an uniformity of deſign, and juſtneſs of arrangement, that ought to ſhame his pretended imitator.

(*b*) " Is there a paſſage" (he aſks) " which panders to the pol-" luted affections and paſſions of bad men ?" A pretty bold challenge ! Have you then, my good Sir, never chanced to hear of a *gentle, amiable* paſſion called—Envy ? Or are Men of Letters and

Authors

Indignant virtue yet fhall mark thy fhame,
And juftice blot thee from the rolls of fame.　　300

Thus fafhion's praife allured the Sat'rift's lay
To trifling themes that perifh with the day,
Bade him to fleeting modes adapt his mind,
Nor trace the bolder features of mankind;
And thus keen ridicule, which, well applied,
Checks full-blown arrogance and upftart pride,
Infpired by (c) felf-conceit, at random throws
It's wanton fhafts, confounding friends with foes.

　　　　　　　　　　　　　　　　　　　But

Authors peculiarly exempt from it? What fay you then to a work, in which almoft every Reader, efpecially if alfo an Author, may find fome enemy, fome rival, or fome envied fuperior, depreciated or ridiculed? What fay you to a work, in which the flighteft failings in men of talents and virtue are eagerly feized and invidioufly amplified? in which the private concerns of Authors are brought forward merely to render them objects of contempt? in which the motives of public exertion are mifreprefented, and the zeal of benevolence laughed to fcorn? But, independent of this confideration, let me afk, is the general curiofity and appetite for flander among the paffions moft *honourable* to human nature? The boaft of having publifhed nothing offenfive to female delicacy is equally unfounded. See the paffages cited in *Strictures on the Purfuits of Literature,* and thofe referred to in this Work. Some others might be mentioned.

(c) It would, furely, be fuperfluous to quote inftances of conceit in the little Satirift. It pervades his whole work. He muft have

　　　　　　　　　　　　　　　　　　　　　　rigid

But you, ye candid few, whofe generous praife
Can beam on merit's unprefuming lays,   310
Whom facred truth can charm, whom heaven has
    graced
With native fenfe, with independent tafte,
Affert your facred rights! fulfil your truft!
And, fpurning fafhion's fway, ftill dare be juft!
Nor you, ye injured Bards! who fcorn to pay
Bafe homage to the minion of the day,
Retort his fneering profe, or flippant rhyme,
But calmly wait the juft award of time.
Britain, at length awaked, fhall own your claim,
Shall yield the full, the lafting meed of fame,   320
And ftamp with juft applaufe your honeft page,
Secured from envy's hate and faction's rage.

rigid mufcles from whom the felf-importance of this " ftrutting
" Bantam" does not frequently provoke a fmile. What, for inftance, can be more truly ridiculous than his citing, on the authority of his fingle affertion, four gentlemen as admiring his book, not
one of whom has *publifhed* a fyllable concerning it. We have often
feen teftimonies of diftinguifhed writers quoted in recommendation
of a work. But this, perhaps, is the firft inftance of an anonymous
writer affuring the world that fuch and fuch men of literature com-
mend his book. But as he is fo fond of private anecdotes, let me
advife him not to boaft too much of Mr. Storer's " *love to his*
" *Lines* ;" as thereby hangs a tale. Mr. S., on whofe praife he
plumes himfelf, laid a trap for the GREAT AUTHOR's vanity, and
fuccceded to a miracle. Never was a man of fuch *profound* wifdom
fo compleatly duped.

POSTSCRIPT.

THE little Satirift appearing confcious of the indignation excited by his brutal attack on Dr. Warton, and attempting to juftify it, a more full difcuffion of that fubjeƈt may not be improper; though (as the public mind is pretty well made up on his conduƈt) it may not be neceffary. It has, indeed, been ably treated by the author of *Striƈtures on the Purfuits of Literature*; but to perfons who have not feen that work, the following confiderations will, I think, fhew the artifices and malignity of our Satirift in their true light.

1. Nothing, when duly confidered, can be more captious than to cenfure an Editor for publifhing a likenefs of his author. It is not, indeed, abfolutely neceffary; but cuftom authorizes and in fome degree requires it; and it gratifies a very natural and harmlefs curiofity. Why then fhould a praƈtice encouraged in others, be cenfured in Lord Sheffield and Dr. Warton? Becaufe, forfooth, Gibbon had a clumfy perfon, and Pope a deformed one!—As if the knowledge of thefe circumftances could leffen the fame of either of thofe diftinguifhed writers! The likenefs of Pope was taken by an eminent painter without the leaft view to caricature, and certainly makes him lefs deformed than tradition had reprefented him. But were it otherwife, what injury could be done thereby to his memory? What can it take from that reputation which was gained by the qualities of his mind, not of his perfon?

2. Another

2. Another objection is, that Dr. Warton has borrowed many of the notes from his celebrated Essay. But would any man professing to give an edition of Pope, with compleat Notes, have done otherwise? Had Dr. W. avoided every remark that had appeared in his Essay, what censure would he not then have incurred! Should we not have been told that, from interested motives (namely, that his Essay might still be an object of purchase), he had, in the edition, presented us with the mere refuse of his brain, with the gleanings of a harvest already gathered? And how many Critics would have lamented that some other person had not undertaken the task, who would, without scruple, have borrowed the most valuable remarks from Dr. Warton, since the Doctor would not from himself!

3. On the next ground of attack, I am sensible that Dr. W. may be defended with great appearance of reason. This has been ably performed by the author of *Strictures on The Pursuits of Literature.* I am sensible that here too the little Satirist has been guilty of a misrepresentation; for Poems published by Pope himself, or with his consent, in his riper years, are very different from Mr. E.'s *Geranium,* or any other irregular sally of youth never published by it's author. Neither is Warburton's edition free from objectionable passages, and even poems. Yet I admit that, as far as my own opinion goes, it might have been better if Dr. W. had not so strictly interpreted his duty as an Editor. But did that error, if it be one, require such a profusion of insults and invectives? Is it true, as the Satirist asserts, that the *edition* only, not the *editor,* is the object of his animadversion? Let any reader turn to the eight lines of the Text (I am ashamed to recite them) in which so many opprobrious epithets are lavished! Let him turn even to the Note that contains this

assertion,

aſſertion, and ſay there is no unprovoked and unneceſſary perſonality! No man, I repeat it, who had the feelings of a man, would have raked out ſo induſtriouſly, and aggravated ſo groſsly, every little blemiſh in Dr. W.'s work; or would have inſulted by ſuch language a man of his age and character. But no reſpect (it ſeems) is due to *age!* No, not even in the caſe of an eminent and amiable perſon! Have you forgotten then (moſt *worthy* ſir) the maxims of all your favourite claſſics? "*It is not* (you tell us) *in the title* "*page*"—Pro pudor!—Is there a ſingle reader of ſuch a book ignorant that Dr. Warton has been for nearly half a century one of the brighteſt ornaments to the claſſical literature of his country? But charge muſt be heaped upon charge. A few general obſervations (perfectly accordant with the ſpirit of the conſtitution) are picked out and diſtorted from their true meaning, in order to prove (contrary to the tenor of his work and life) Dr. W. a favourer of democracy. This, I am confident, is the firſt time ſuch a charge has been even inſinuated againſt him. His bittereſt enemies (if he has. enemies) would be aſhamed of it. But "*Cæſar aſhamed!*" No: that quality of the mind has not a name in his vocabu-, lary, not a correſpondent feeling in his breaſt. If, however, indignation at malignity would permit one to ſmile at the inconſiſtencies of ſelf-conceit, it would be amuſing to ſee the man who above all writers (of any learning) deals in colloquial. barbariſms and vulgar idioms, reproaching Dr. Warton with what he is pleaſed to term vulgarity. Would it be believed that, in the work of this Cenſor General, of this faſtidious hypercritic, may be found ſuch couplets as this:

He *roſe*, late heeded by patrician care,
Though private friendſhip *help'd him to the chair!*

(N.B. This jumble of incongruity and vulgarity very *judiciouſly* cloſes a laboured paſſage.)

Or